A BLUE BANNER
BIOGRAPHY

Chris Brown

Kathleen Tracy

P.O. Box 196
Hockessin, Delaware 19707
Visit us on the web: www.mitchelllane.com
Comments? email us: mitchelllane@mitchelllane.com

Mitchell Lane PUBLISHERS

Printing   1   2   3   4   5   6   7   8   9

Blue Banner Biographies

Akon	Alan Jackson	Alicia Keys
Allen Iverson	Ashanti	Ashlee Simpson
Ashton Kutcher	Avril Lavigne	Bernie Mac
Beyoncé	Bow Wow	Britney Spears
Carrie Underwood	**Chris Brown**	Chris Daughtry
Christina Aguilera	Christopher Paul Curtis	Ciara
Clay Aiken	Condoleezza Rice	Daniel Radcliffe
David Ortiz	Derek Jeter	Eminem
Eve	Fergie (Stacy Ferguson)	50 Cent
Gwen Stefani	Ice Cube	Jamie Foxx
Ja Rule	Jay-Z	Jennifer Lopez
Jessica Simpson	J. K. Rowling	Johnny Depp
JoJo	Justin Berfield	Justin Timberlake
Kate Hudson	Keith Urban	Kelly Clarkson
Kenny Chesney	Lance Armstrong	Lindsay Lohan
Mariah Carey	Mario	Mary J. Blige
Mary-Kate and Ashley Olsen	Michael Jackson	Miguel Tejada
Missy Elliott	Nancy Pelosi	Nelly
Orlando Bloom	P. Diddy	Paris Hilton
Peyton Manning	Queen Latifah	Ron Howard
Rudy Giuliani	Sally Field	Selena
Shakira	Shirley Temple	Tim McGraw
Usher	Zac Efron	

Library of Congress Cataloging-in-Publication Data
Tracy, Kathleen.
  Chris Brown / by Kathleen Tracy.
    p. cm. — (Blue banner biographies)
  Includes bibliographical references, discography (p.   ), filmography (p.   ), and index.
  ISBN 978-1-58415-617-8 (library bound)
  1. Brown, Chris, 1989– —Juvenile literature. 2. Rap musicians—United States—Biography—Juvenile literature. I. Title.
  ML3930.B865T73 2008
  782.421649092—dc22
  [B]
                                                                                        2007019783

ABOUT THE AUTHOR: Kathleen Tracy has been a journalist for over twenty years. Her writing has been featured in magazines including *The Toronto Star's Star Week*, *A&E Biography* magazine, *KidScreen* and *Variety*. She is also the author of numerous biographies and other nonfiction books, including *Mariano Guadalupe Vallejo*, *William Hewlett: Pioneer of the Computer Age*, *The Watergate Scandal*, *The Life and Times of Cicero*, *Mariah Carey*, *Kelly Clarkson*, and *The Plymouth Colony: The Pilgrims Settle in New England* for Mitchell Lane Publishers. She divides her time between homes in Studio City and Palm Springs, California.

PHOTO CREDITS: Cover, p. 4—Fitzroy Barrett/Globe Photos; p. 6—Frazer Harrison/Getty Images; pp. 11, 24—Frank Micelotta/Getty Images; p. 12—Barry Talesnick/Globe Photos; p. 15—Nina Prommer/Globe Photos; p. 16—Chris Brown/Jive Records; p. 19—Scott Gries/Getty Images; p. 20—Kevin Winter/Getty Images; p. 26—Mat Szwajkos/Getty Images; p. 27—Ed Geller/Globe Photos.

PUBLISHER'S NOTE: The following story has been thoroughly researched, and to the best of our knowledge represents a true story. While every possible effort has been made to ensure accuracy, the publisher will not assume liability for damages caused by inaccuracies in the data, and makes no warranty on the accuracy of the information contained herein. This story has not been authorized or endorsed by Chris Brown.

PLB

CONTENTS

In 2006, Chris Brown won an NAACP Image Award. Known for his love of fashion, the singer and actor hopes to start an affordable clothing line for kids who want to be stylish but don't have a lot of money to spend.

The New Usher . . . NOT!

Moments before the show begins, the audience is restless. The murmurs of anticipation create a low buzz, like a circling swarm of bees looking for a place to land. Some of the young girls in the audience look as though they'll burst into tears if they have to wait one minute longer. Finally, Chris Brown and his eight backup dancers explode onto the stage, and the arena erupts in a deafening roar of squeals, screams, and cheers.

For the next hour, Brown captivates the audience with his smooth voice and athletic dance moves that include leaps, somersaults, and back flips, eliciting even louder applause. Tall and lanky, Brown struts across the stage confidently but makes a point to engage his audience with lots of eye contact while flashing his killer smile. Brown serenades two starstruck, overwhelmed girls plucked from the audience. They look as if they will faint at any moment.

In addition to performing the songs from his wildly successful first album, Brown also pays musical homage to

At the 2006 BET Awards, where he won Best New Artist and Viewer's Choice honors, Chris wowed the audience with his singing and smooth moves. Although he never took dance lessons, Brown is known for his high-energy concerts.

one of his heroes, Michael Jackson. The crowd goes crazy when Chris pulls on a sequined glove and moonwalks.

For the entire hour, the audience never stops cheering. The applause continues long after Brown takes his final curtain call and heads back to the dressing room.

For teenage R&B sensation Chris Brown, it's just another amazing day in what has been an amazing two years.

He's been called—repeatedly—the "new" Usher. While Brown understands such well-intentioned comparisons are compliments of the highest order, he wants to be known for his own unique style and personality.

"I think [Usher's] the real deal," Brown said in the *Los Angeles Times.* "There aren't many popular teenage boys singing who can connect with teen girls. . . . At the end of the day, I'm seventeen and I'm a young dude with a lot of respect for him. With Usher growing up, there's a new kid on the block who can sing and dance."

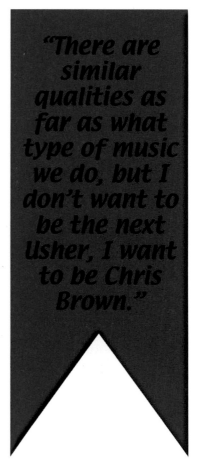

"There are similar qualities as far as what type of music we do, but I don't want to be the next Usher, I want to be Chris Brown."

That said, Brown admitted to writer J. Freedom du Lac, "So many people compare me to him, and I don't think it'll ever stop. I'm not gonna say that I hate it, because I really respect Usher and I was influenced by him. But I want people to see me for me—not just the next whoever. Not a clone. I just want to be recognized as being my own person and as being a unique artist in the game.

"There are similar qualities as far as what type of music we do, but I don't want to be the next Usher, I want to be Chris Brown."

What Brown doesn't mind is his Usher-like appeal to women. "That's what drives me in the show," he told

Kamal Larsuel. "That's what I love. I love attention. I just go out there and jump onstage and if I see a gang of girls? That makes me just dance even more.

"It's like when you're in the mall with your boys and you try to be flyer than all of them so you can get a girl. Or you're at a basketball game and you see the cheerleader or the girls in the bleachers — you're gonna try to show off just a little bit.

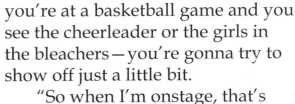

"So when I'm onstage, that's what makes me show off a little bit more. Just do my dances a little bit harder and go after it a little bit harder. Go at 110 percent."

While comfortable with his success, Brown admitted to *Teen People* he's still surprised by it. "That's why I'm happy every day. It never was like, *Yeah, I knew this was coming.* I had an idea that it might, but I didn't know what my potential was at all. And I didn't know that people were going to believe in me as an artist and as an actor, so I definitely look at it as a blessing," he said. "I'm just taking it day by day. I'm enjoying being able to travel and I can't wait to get onstage. As long as I touch the stage, I'm happy."

His incentive to keep working hard is simple. "Don't mess it up or God will take it away."

There's little chance of that for someone with talent that clearly seems heaven-sent.

Small-town Boy, Big-time Dreams

*C*hristopher Maurice Brown was born on May 5, 1989, in Tappahannock, Virginia. Tappahannock was given its name by Captain John Smith, who came upon the area in 1608 after helping settle the colony at Jamestown. Smith had set off to map the coastal lands in and around Chesapeake Bay. When he reached a river about fifty miles north of where Williamsburg would later be settled, Smith was prevented from landing by an unwelcoming tribe of natives from a nearby village.

Smith called the river Rappahannock, which is a Native American word meaning "ebb and flow of water," and the village Tappahannock, which means "town on the water that ebbs and flows."

With only around 2,000 residents, Tappahannock isn't all that much bigger now than it was back then. So small that it has only one grade school—Tappahannock Elementary—the town is a picturesque community that is proud of its history and deep American roots. Several buildings from colonial times remain and have become popular tourist attractions.

Growing up in Tappahannock, Chris was practically dancing before he could even walk. "When I was two, I knew I was bound to do something in entertainment," he claimed in *Jet*. "I was dancing and watching TV and seeing people like Michael Jackson. It just came to me, and from that point on, I was always dancing."

He told Kamal Larsuel, "I had all of the routines down and everything and I was like, *That's who I want to be like*."

> Chris has "always felt the hate in my heart for anybody that disrespected a lady or called a lady the 'B' word."

Brown frequently credits his parents for developing his appreciation of music because they were always listening to R&B on the radio. He has rarely talked in detail about his family life when growing up, but he admitted in a 2006 MTV interview that his dad, Clinton, and his mom, Joyce Hawkins, had a troubled marriage.

"I had a father that used to abuse my mom when I was seven or eight," he said. Chris and his older sister, Lytrell, "used to tell my mom, 'Why are you staying with him?'" Even though his parents eventually divorced, the experience was so traumatic that Brown says he has "always felt the hate in my heart for anybody that disrespected a lady or called a lady the 'B' word."

One of Brown's idols is Michael Jackson. At the 2006 World Music Awards in London, Chris paid homage to Jackson by performing "Thriller."

For a while, Chris went to stay with his aunt in Arkansas. While there, he and his cousins would perform together in local talent shows. Back in Tappahannock, he was cast in the lead role for his third-grade Christmas show. But his first dream wasn't to become a singer; it was to be a rapper. "I grew up in this little country town that nobody ever got out of and made it big," he said on RepVideo.com. "I wanted to be the first MC out of Tappahannock."

Brown says he started taking singing seriously when he was eleven after his mom nudged him in that direction.

"I was rapping," he says on his Web site, "and didn't understand that I could sing . . . my mom heard me singing around the house and said, '*What are you doing? You really can sing!*'"

Brown always makes time for his fans, like the ones he met during the 2006 Macy's Thanksgiving Day Parade. He thinks it is important for artists to be good role models for their young fans. He encourages kids to stay in school and to treat each other with respect.

Joyce took her son to church so that he could sing in the choir, but what really caught Chris's attention was the idea that he could impress girls with his voice. "My mom said girls love singers," he told TeenPeople.com, "so I went to school and started singing to girls."

Chris admits it was a revelation. "The girls . . . were feeling me," he said in *USA Today.* "That's when I knew I could do this and I knew that I wanted to have a music career."

Fate was on his side. Chris says he hooked up with a local production company after "they met my father at a gas station and they said they were looking for talent."

Chris's life was about to change forever.

Learning the Ropes

Pursuing his dream of being a performer meant leaving Tappahannock—his friends, his place on his high school basketball team, his family . . . at least for a while. Chris's production team took him to New York, where for the next year and a half he worked with songwriters while his team tried to get him a record deal.

Brown admits the pace of New York and the temperament of its citizens took some getting used to. "When you come to New York for the first time, you really have to get accustomed to it," he told AllHipHop.com.

"You have to have a certain swagger growing up in the streets. It's a whole different attitude . . . the way you carry yourself is totally different than in Tappahannock. You . . . try to avoid different situations; dudes think you're in a gang; dudes want to fight you; dudes even try to end your life.

"So I just stayed to myself and did what I had to do. I tried to grind out and do my music. I really wasn't shocked at the way of New York; it is what it is. It was still enjoyable.

"I acquired street smarts and learned from a lot of things and grew from it."

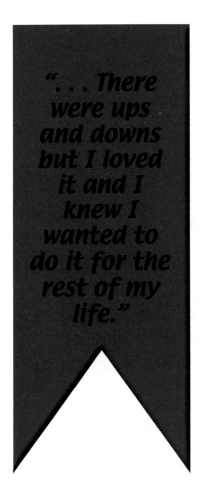

"... There were ups and downs but I loved it and I knew I wanted to do it for the rest of my life."

Chris recalled that as the months passed, there were times "I doubted myself. But I never fell back or took steps back. In my head it was always about taking steps forward, taking it higher and higher. There were ups and downs but I loved it and I knew I wanted to do it for the rest of my life."

Eventually his effort paid off the day Tina Davis, an executive at Def Jam Records, was listening to a demo with songs from several different artists on it. Chris's singing immediately stood out. "I picked Chris out of the seven acts because of his voice," she later told *Pollstar*.

Davis arranged to meet Chris. "When he came to my office, he was a little nervous. He performed for me, then I had him perform for a couple of people in the office."

Each time Chris sang, he kept getting better—good enough that Davis took him to see the head of the label, legendary music producer LA Reid. "Chris blew everybody away in the room."

Brown was equally impressed with Davis. "At first, I thought the record label would be real big snobby people," he admitted. "But she was real nice and down-to-earth. I

Even though he once wanted to be a rapper, Brown says the rap he grew up with has changed — he believes for the worse. He doesn't like the glorification of drugs, violence, and disrespect of women he hears in today's rap.

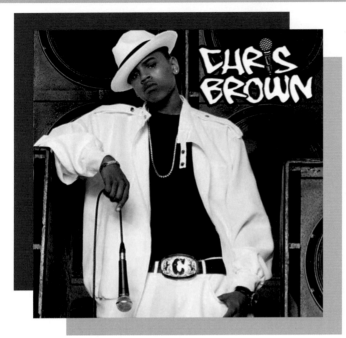

Just one month after its release, Brown's debut album, Chris Brown, *had sold over a million copies.*

started to believe what she was saying so by the time she took me to see LA Reid, I felt confident enough to perform my best. It was exciting."

Davis was convinced and got the paperwork under way to sign Brown. Unfortunately, before the deal could be finalized, she lost her job when Def Jam merged with another label.

Rather than see the experience as a bitter disappointment, Chris turned it into a positive. The day after Tina Davis left Def Jam, he asked her to be his manager. She agreed.

"We would sit down and talk about his ideas and his thoughts and that's when I realized he's one hundred percent an artist," Davis said.

Her first priority was finding Chris a record deal. By December 2004, she had three different record labels making offers. In the end, Chris signed with Jive Records, which also handled Britney Spears and Justin Timberlake. Chris and his mom moved to New Jersey, and Chris got ready to start recording his first album. Over the next six months he recorded nearly fifty songs; he and Davis would select fifteen to go on the album.

Chris loved traveling to different cities to work with different producers. "It was hard," he told *KidzWorld*, "but it was fun at the same time."

Up to then, Chris had very little experience performing live. Davis put him on a crash course, coaching him on everything from interacting with the audience to the proper way to hold a microphone. By the time he put on a special showcase in May 2005, Brown was a polished, confident performer.

No wonder that in the album's liner notes, Brown wrote, "Thank you! God, God, God, God, God."

He was also a phenomenon. The single "Run It!" was released around Chris's sixteenth birthday. It zoomed up the charts all the way to number one, where it stayed for five weeks. The song became the biggest debut single by a male in the history of the Billboard Hot 100.

His album *Chris Brown* was released in November 2005 and within a month had sold over half a million copies. It would go on to be certified double platinum and be the number-one album on both the R&B and hip-hop charts. No wonder that in the album's liner notes, Brown wrote, "Thank you! God, God, God, God, God."

Now came the hard part—proving he wasn't a one-hit wonder.

Runnin' It

*I*n December 2005, Chris went on his first series of live performances as part of the HollaDay Jam Tour. The response was overwhelming.

"When his backdrop went off the girls just started screaming and continued to scream until he got off the stage," Tina Davis reported to *Pollstar*. "We'd be driving down the freeway and people would be blowing their horns trying to pull us over to sign autographs. After every show we'd have to get a police escort because the girls wouldn't let the bus go."

Suddenly, Chris couldn't go anywhere without being recognized. While shopping for Christmas presents back home in Virginia, he literally had to run out of the shopping mall. "People were trying to run up and grab me," he recalled. "I didn't want to be rude, but the whole mall was following me."

Brown thinks part of his appeal is that he respects women and believes in being a gentleman. "I look forward

The one downside of Chris's success is that his hectic work schedule leaves little time for dating. One thing he does make time for is helping others, such as taking part in the Saving OurSelves "BET Relief Telethon." The fund-raiser was to aid victims of Hurricane Katrina.

to growing into [a sex symbol] but I'm not trying to be one right away. I don't want to be too kiddie, but I don't want to be too grown, either. This gives me time to grow with my audience so that I can make that change when I'm about twenty."

That said, he made sure to point out, "I *do* have abs. But I won't be like, *Wow, I'm going to take my shirt off and oil my body up.* I'm not that type of dude. I'm just trying to . . . be an artist."

He was also trying to balance that with schoolwork. Davis stressed that Chris's education was just as important as his career. "You look at stories about teenage kids growing up too fast in the industry," she said. "I think because of past experiences, [record labels] are really

Chris doesn't take the label of sex symbol too seriously, saying he doesn't want to grow up that fast. Although he works out and takes pride in his developing physique, he is content to take his time making the transition from teen idol to adult heartthrob. But when he performed at the Grammy Awards in February 2007, it was clear that Chris was no young kid anymore.

equipped now for young artists to get through it and still get their education."

For Chris that meant a tutor who toured with him throughout 2006 and assigned daily homework, just as if he were still in school. "I try to do all that I can to be a role model, showing kids that it is cool to get an education," Chris said.

Still, most of the time his day revolves around making music. "I get up in the morning, work out. After that, I do certain business things at Jive. If I have a show that day, I get ready for the show. And then basically try to rest my vocals."

As he told music critic Melissa Ruggieri, "I don't really ever get a day off, we're on the road so much. We might have one rest day. When I'm not performing, I'm playing basketball and trying to have fun.

"I still bring PlayStation Two and Xbox on the road. My dancers are like my brothers; we dance, laugh and play around."

When he's back home in Virginia, Chris says, "My personal life is the same." He hangs with

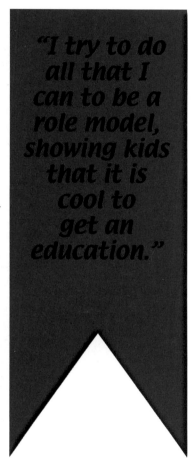

"I try to do all that I can to be a role model, showing kids that it is cool to get an education."

"friends . . . that I used to go to high school with. They're my homies so I just chill with them whenever I'm back home.

"At the end of the day, this is just a job. I love what I do, and it's a great job. But it's like my alter ego. There's Chris Brown the singer. And there's Christopher Brown, the down-home Tappahannock boy that plays video games and basketball and hangs out."

And who thinks about girls. A lot. It's about the only thing that can distract him from singing and dancing.

"The number one thing that takes my focus away is girls," he admitted to Kamal Larsuel. "If I see a room full of girls, I'm not going to be able to focus on what they want me to do. I'm gonna go in that room, *Hey, how y'all doin'?*"

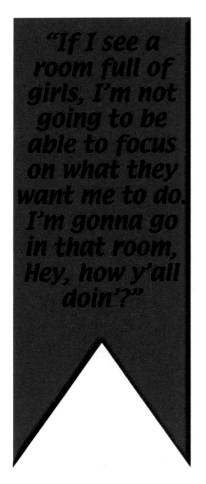

"If I see a room full of girls, I'm not going to be able to focus on what they want me to do. I'm gonna go in that room, Hey, how y'all doin'?"

He laments that his schedule has made it next to impossible to go on a date, much less have a full-time girlfriend. "My schedule is nonstop so the date might be five to ten minutes long," he told TeenHollywood.com. "I like smart girls, a sense of humor but at the same time, I like aggressive ladies."

What he doesn't like is the way rap has changed. "I wouldn't go back to my rapping because nowadays it's different," he told the *Richmond Times-Dispatch* in August 2006. "I'm not going to brag about selling drugs and shooting people and other stuff. That's dumb. I mean, I don't even respect half of that."

Brown says he doesn't drink or do drugs, preferring to get his high from sports like basketball, martial arts, and boxing.

And from his new passion—acting.

An All-around Performer

*C*hris's outgoing personality and popularity weren't lost on Hollywood, and soon the acting offers were coming. He had a guest appearance as himself on the TV series *One on One*, where he sang his top-ten hit "Yo (Excuse Me Miss)." Then Brown made his feature film debut in *Stomp the Yard*, which is about a Los Angeles street dancer.

Brown admitted in *Jet* that his first day on the set was nerve-wracking. "I didn't know if everyone was going to be one hundred percent nice because you hear stories about getting yelled at or kicked off the set. . . . But when I got there, everybody was like family. Everybody was happy. They were cool and just chillin' so I was cool."

Then, in the middle of his second tour, Chris was offered a recurring role on *The O.C.* He openly admits it's his success as a singer that has given him the opportunity to act, but he also points out, "It's not like people say it's like — that rappers and singers get the roles easy because of who they are. Yes, you get roles because of your status, but

Brown filmed the music video for "Gimme That" at Los Angeles's Union Station in 2006. Since then, his acting career has taken off.

at the same time you have to prove to the director or the producer that you can do it; otherwise you won't get the part. If you can't pull it off, they are not going to be able to use you."

In early 2007, Chris began filming his biggest role yet, in the feature film *This Christmas.* "I was a little skeptical," he admitted to TeenHollywood.com, "because I was still balancing my album trying to get everything done." When the producer agreed to work around Brown's recording schedule, Chris accepted the part.

"I really want to show other talents that I'm born with. But, right now, my music and my acting is gonna be totally different. My acting name is going to probably be Christopher Brown or Christopher Maurice and then my singing, I'm just going to keep Chris Brown.

"Then I'm just gonna let the audience decide. That's what makes a hundred percent of everything work anyway; the audience. They buy. They're the consumer. I'm just going to say, when they see me in a movie, I think they're gonna be surprised. I really didn't have too many acting coaches. In my first movie, I didn't have an acting coach. On this movie, I really didn't have one. It's just me, all natural, just trying to show my ability."

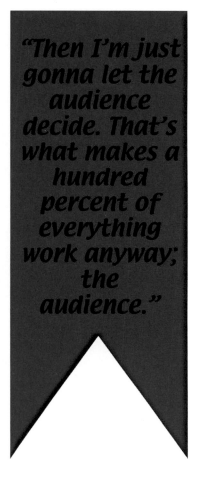

"Then I'm just gonna let the audience decide. That's what makes a hundred percent of everything work anyway; the audience."

Meanwhile, he was working on his second album, *Exclusive.* It was scheduled for release in 2007.

Another goal he has is to create a Chris Brown clothing line that most kids can afford to buy. "I wasn't middle-class, I was poor, so I know how people are when they go shopping. If they see me rockin' something and it's cheap, then *bam*—that's good for them."

Once he turned eighteen, Chris no longer had tutors, nor did his mother go on tour with him. "She traveled with me the first two years so she was around putting down the regulation. But now that I'm becoming more mature, she's let me be a man and make my own mistakes."

So far, he doesn't seem to be making many. Brown says he's "just trying to stay positive and not getting sidetracked;

Chris has always enjoyed playing basketball, so he jumped at the chance to join VH1's 2006 Hip Hop Honors Celebrity Hoops in Brooklyn, New York. The money raised by the event benefited the Madison Square Boys and Girls Club.

just focusing on what's at hand. I have a wide range of fans. . . . It's great to know that I have people like that who look up to me. It means that I have a bigger job and a bigger calling that God has sent me on, so I know what to do. I'm really glad, really thankful that I'm in this position now to be a mentor and to influence younger kids to be themselves, to be individuals and think positively.

"I don't want to let anyone down."

His desire to be there for people is why he didn't hesitate when contacted by the Make-A-Wish Foundation to visit a three-year-old girl suffering from leukemia. The fact that his music could touch kids that young was a surprise. "I was, like, I know certain kids listen to me but a three-year-old, that's wild!"

His biggest goal, he says, is to "put Tappahannock on the map. I want to give all those people in small towns

Chris was a big winner at the 2006 Billboard Music Awards. He was honored as Male Artist of the Year, New Artist of the Year, and Artist of the Year. He has also shown he has talent beyond singing. He codirected his music videos "Yo" and "Gimme That," cowrote a dozen songs on his second album (Exclusive), *and has acted in the movie* Stomp the Yard *and the TV series* The O.C.

hope—you don't have to be from New York or L.A. or Atlanta to make it in music or to follow your dream."

Although success has certainly given Chris the freedom to live anywhere he wants, he still makes Tappahannock his home. Fame, he says, "doesn't limit you, but you have to be cautious. . . . I just see myself as a regular dude doing what I love, being able to show my fans what I'm capable of doing as well as touching my fans with my music. I'm just a boy from Tappahannock, Virginia, and from there followed my dream."

All the way to the top.

CHRONOLOGY

1989 Christopher Maurice Brown is born May 5 in
Tappahannock, Virginia.

2003 At the age of fourteen, Chris moves to New York to
work on demo tapes.

2004 He signs with Jive Records in December.

2005 Chris's single "Run It!" is released in July, and his debut
album, *Chris Brown,* is released in November.

2006 *Chris Brown* is certified platinum in January. Chris wins
NAACP Image Award for Outstanding New Artist in
February; Soul Train Music Award for Best New R&B/
Soul Artist in March; BET Award for Best New Artist in
June; Teen Choice Award for Music Breakout Male in
August; and Billboard Awards for Male Artist of the
Year, New Artist of the Year, and Artist of the Year in
December.

2007 Chris appears in his first feature film, *Stomp the Yard,* as
well as in three episodes of *The O.C.* He releases his
second album, *Exclusive,* and costars in the film *This
Christmas.*

Albums

2007 *Exclusive*

2005 *Chris Brown*

Hit Singles

2007 "Wall to Wall"

2005 "Run It!"

"Yo (Excuse Me Miss)"

"Gimme That"

"Say Goodbye"

"Poppin'"

2007 *Stomp the Yard*

The O.C. (TV series)

After School

This Christmas

2006 *Christmas in Washington* (TV special)

Chris Brown's Journey (concert documentary film)

FURTHER READING

For Young Readers

"Five Questions for: Chris Brown." *Ebony.* June 1, 2006.

Hooper, James. *Chris Brown.* Broomall, Pennsylvania: Mason Crest Publishers, 2006.

Works Consulted

Access All Areas: *Chris Brown,* "Interview"
http://www.accessallareas.net.au/artists/
Chris_Brown.php#interview

Amendola, Tina. "Chris Brown"
http://www.pollstar.com/news/viewhotstar.pl?Artist=CHSBRO

Barker, Lynn. *Interviews,* "Chris Brown: On the Set of His New Film!" http://www.teenhollywood.com/d/142839/1038/
chris-brown-on-the-set-of-his-new-film.html

Du Lac, J. Freedom. "Running with It." *The Washington Post.*
December 29, 2005, p. C1.

Guzman, Rafer. "Heartthrob Offers Brief Summary of His Life."
Chicago Tribune. April 26, 2006, p. 7.

Jones, Steve. "He's in No Hurry to 'Run It.' " *USA Today,* December 13, 2005.

KidzWorld: "Chris Brown Interview,"
http://www.kidzworld.com/article/5970-chris-brown-interview

Larsuel, Kamal. "The Diva's Interview with Chris Brown," January 12, 2007, http://www.3blackchicks.com// index.php?option=com_content&task=view&id=821&Itemid=30

MSNBC: *Access Hollywood,* "Chris Brown a Hero to Three-year-old Cancer Patient," http://www.msnbc.msn.com/id/13211345/

Nand, Ashlene. *Alternatives,* "Chris Brown: New Kid on the Block" http://www.allhiphop.com/Alternatives/?ID=226

Rap Video: "Artist: Chris Brown," http://www.rapvideo.com/artists/view/11.html

Ruggieri, Melissa. *Entertainment & Weekend,* "The Beat: He's Got a Way with Life" http://www.timesdispatch.com/servlet/ Satellite?pagename=RTD/MGArticle/ RTD_BasicArticle&c=MGArticle&cid=1149190147577

Sanneh, Kelefa. "Crooning and Rap, in Harmony." *The New York Times,* November 24, 2005.

Waldron, Clarence. "Fresh Faces in R&B Music." *Jet,* May 29, 2006.

You Tube: "Chris Brown Interview" http://www.youtube.com/watch?v=iBgDCw9iHJk

Online
Chris Brown — Jive Records
http://www.chrisbrownworld.com

Chris Brown on MySpace
http://www.myspace.com/chrisbrown

Chris Brown on TagWorld
http://www.tagworld.com/chrisbrown

Chris Brown Web
http://www.chrisbrownweb.com

INDEX